Collective Biographies

AFRICAN-AMERICAN POETS

Michael R. Strickland

E **Enslow Publishers, Inc.**
44 Fadem Road   PO Box 38
Box 699   Aldershot
Springfield, NJ 07081   Hants GU12 6BP
USA   UK

To Father Ed Bradley, and the English Department
of Seton Hall Prep

Copyright © 1996 by Michael R. Strickland

Library of Congress Cataloging-in-Publication Data

Strickland, Michael R.
    African-American poets / Michael R. Strickland.
        p. cm. — (Collective biographies)
    Includes bibliographical references and index.
    Summary: Profiles the lives and work of ten African American poets:
Gwendolyn Brooks, Haki R. Madhubuti, Rita Dove, Eloise Greenfield,
Langston Hughes, Imamu Amiri Baraka, Maya Angelou, Paul Laurence
Dunbar, and Nikki Giovanni.
    ISBN 0-89490-774-3
    1. Afro-American poets—Biography—Juvenile literature. 2. American
poetry—Afro-American authors—History and criticism—Juvenile literature.
[1. Poets, American. 2. Afro-Americans—biography. 3. American poetry—
Afro-American authors.] I. Title. II. Series.
PS153.N5S77 1996
811.009'896073—dc20   96-2016
                                  CIP
Printed in the United States of America.   AC

10 9 8 7 6 5 4 3 2 1

Illustration Credits: Dwight Carter, p. 74; Barron Claiborne, p. 64;
Contemporary Forum, p. 38; Corbis-Bettmann, pp. 10, 18; Risasi Dais, p. 46;
Used by Permission of Eloise Greenfield, p. 82; Springer/Corbis-Bettmann,
p. 28; Third World Press, p. 54; Fred Viebahn, 90.

Cover Illustration: AP/Wide World Photos

Contents

Introduction

black man, quit stuttering and shuffling, look up
black man, quit whining and stooping, for all of him
For Great Malcolm a prince of the earth, let
nothing in us rest
until we avenge ourselves of his death.

"A Poem For Black Hearts"
—by Amiri Baraka

The shooting of civil rights leader Malcolm X in 1965 provided a focal point of rage for Amiri Baraka, a leading poet of the Black Arts movement. The Black Arts movement was the literary and cultural wing of the Black Power struggle. In the 1960s, the Civil Rights movement was at its peak. Along with it came new ways of thinking about African Americans. A strong sense of African-American identity began to emerge. African-American novelist Ishmael Reed called the sixties "the decade that screamed."

The Black Arts movement served two functions that are significant to African Americans today. First, important African-American texts that had been ignored were discovered. Second, black literature was defined in terms that were different from those used for works by white writers. Black Arts supporters sought forms and themes that arose from the context of African-American culture and were their own frame of reference. This became known as Black Aesthetic theory. It generated a remarkable amount of criticism and theory about African-American literature.

African-American poetry did not start in the 1960s, however. It began in the 1700s, when most African Americans were in slavery. Phillis Wheatley is considered the greatest colonial African-American poet. An African-born slave, Wheatley was among the few African Americans allowed to read and write in the 1700s. In her lifetime, she was celebrated throughout the United States and Europe, yet she died alone and in poverty. The quality of Wheatley's poetry was noted by those who questioned the mental ability of Africans. At that time, many white Americans thought that Africans were inferior. Wheatley's book was published with eighteen endorsements from experts who said that it was indeed the authentic work of a former slave. Learning to read and write was a dangerous act for a slave. Slaveowners feared reading and writing would cause trouble among slaves.

Between the death of Phillis Wheatley in 1784 and the end of the Civil War in 1865, the poetry of African Americans was rarely published. With the end of the war, slavery was abolished. However, many states passed laws that prevented African Americans from having true freedom. Many of these laws kept black and white Americans apart; this practice was called segregation. African Americans were also discriminated against in housing, jobs, and education. They were often not allowed to vote.

In spite of this discrimination, a generation of poets did appear in the 1880s. The sons and daughters of slaves, these poets first imitated the rhyming style of poetry then in fashion. But the boundaries of poetry had already begun to change. Poets were looking at their work in a new way and experimenting with new forms, and some African-American poets began using plantation dialect.

The Harlem Renaissance of the 1920s and 1930s was an explosion of African-American culture. African-American sculptors, artists, musicians, writers, and poets produced an outpouring of work. They formed literary circles and magazines. The 1920s are often referred to as the Jazz Age, because jazz had become the most popular music of the nation. Poet Langston Hughes used the rhythms of jazz in his poetry.

Following the Harlem Renaissance, African Americans continued to produce great works and to break down artistic barriers. In 1950, the poet Gwendolyn Brooks became the first African American to win a Pulitzer Prize for her work. Life for most African Americans, however, was still filled with racism and discrimination. Beginning in the late 1940s, African-American artists began to speak out. They demanded full inclusion in American society.

In the 1960s, many poets began to use poetry to express their political views. Perhaps more forcefully than any other African-American writer, Amiri Baraka has defined the relationship between politics and art. Prior to the Black Arts movement, he was known as LeRoi Jones. By 1959, he was a widely acclaimed poet and playwright. That same year, Langston Hughes wrote him a note: "Hail LeRoi, I hear you are colored." Hughes joked this way because Baraka's early poems barely mentioned race.

Baraka later put the African-American experience at the center of his art, and the Black Arts movement was born. The Black Arts movement swelled the community of African-American readers. Noted scholar Henry Louis Gates, Jr., wrote that this energy spread "from the streets of Harlem to the hallowed halls of Harvard."[1] All sorts of publishers began to print, reprint, and market works by African-American writers. In keeping with the Afrocentric principles of the movement, many African Americans adopted names from Islam, the dominant religion of Western Africa. Jones became Imamu Ameer Baraka. Don Lee, another leader of the Black Arts movement, became Haki Madhubuti. The Nation of Islam, a Muslim group of African Americans, became a powerful force in the Black Power movement. Its most famous spokesperson was Malcolm X.

Poetry celebrating African-American life and

culture became more popular. Some Black Arts poets like Nikki Giovanni turned to writing poetry for children. Many of Giovanni's poems teach children to be proud of their heritage. Some of Eloise Greenfield's poems are classics in children's literature. These include "Honey I Love" and "Nathaniel's Rap." Her poems can be heard in schools across America every day.

The poems of Maya Angelou and Rita Dove express the joys and sorrows of everyday African Americans—from big cities to small towns. Both of these women have also demonstrated the continuing power of African-American poetry. On January 20, 1993, Maya Angelou stood on the steps of the White House to recite a poem she wrote in honor of the inauguration of President Clinton. In that same year, Rita Dove was named Poet Laureate of the United States. This is the highest recognition of a poet by the United States government.

In the two centuries since the death of Phillis Wheatley, African-American poetry has developed into a distinct genre. The ten poets in this book do not represent the complete story of African-American poetry. They are a sample. They are some of the thousands of men and women who use words to paint pictures that tell of the universal emotions felt by all people. African-American poets have used poetry to express the soul of their people. We can follow their example: They capture the heart of a culture and express it now and for the future.

Phillis Wheatley

Phillis Wheatley

(1753–1784)

A slave was brought from Africa to America in 1761. She had no formal education; she was taught only by the master's family. But within sixteen months of her arrival, she had learned the English language. She had been an utter stranger to the language before. When she started reading the most difficult parts of the Bible, she astonished all those who heard her.

Phillis Wheatley was the first African American to publish a book. She was the first American woman to publish a book of poems since Anne Bradstreet had done so in 1650. Wheatley published *Poems on Various Subjects Religious and Moral* in 1773, at the age of nineteen.

Wheatley was purchased in Boston on or about

July 11, 1761. At the time, she was losing her front baby teeth. By this evidence, the year of her birth has been guessed to be 1753. The ship that transported her from Africa was called the *Phillis,* so perhaps she was named after the vessel. Scholars have suggested that Wheatley was born in Gambia. Wheatley described only one memory of Africa, she remembered her mother pouring "out water before the sun at his rising."[1] This life-giving sun became a central image of her poetry, echoing her mother's care. In many of the poems in which this imagery appears, she uses the play on words: sun-Son, comparing the sun to the caring light of Jesus.

After Wheatley was kidnapped in Africa, she was taken to Boston in a slave ship. In 1761 she was sold to John Wheatley, a wealthy tailor. He purchased her for his wife, Susannah, probably as a companion. Phillis was fortunate because Susannah showed sympathy to the young slave girl. "I was treated more like her child than her servant," Wheatley remembered.[2] Wheatley's main biographer, Magaretta Matilda Odell, has recorded an important fact about Wheatley. Shortly after her purchase, the slave girl was often seen trying to make letters on the wall, using a piece of chalk or charcoal.[3] Wheatley quickly became favored and was given a gift known to few slaves: She was taught to read and write.

Mary Wheatley (one of Susannah and John Wheatley's twins; Nathaniel was the other) began to instruct Phillis in reading the English Bible. Phillis

Wheatley also began to learn Latin, mastering enough to read some Latin classics.

Wheatley's first noted piece of writing was a letter that she wrote in 1765 to Samson Occom, a Mohegan minister. Her first poem, which she wrote at about age fourteen, was called, "To the University of Cambridge in New England." Her first published poem—"On Messrs. Hussey and Coffin"—appeared on December 21, 1767, in the *Newport Mercury*. The *Mercury* was a colonial newspaper in Newport, Rhode Island.

Newport was also the home of Phillis Wheatley's African-American friend Obour Tanner. Wheatley and Tanner may have come together from Africa on the slave ship, *Phillis*. In any event, the two frequently wrote letters to each other. Recent evidence suggests that these two visited often as well.

The slave girl must have been one of the most learned young women in Boston. Wheatley was frequently visited by clergymen and other persons who had high standing in Boston society. The colonies' best libraries and better minds were available to Wheatley, so the poet was allowed to develop at her own pace, with little hindrance. There also is evidence that she studied at the singing schools conducted by William Billings, America's first famous composer and choirmaster. Many of the young women Wheatley met at the singing schools were later the subjects of her poems.

John and Susannah Wheatley, who were deeply

committed Christians, thought of Phillis Wheatley as a soul in need of salvation. Phillis Wheatley had two spiritual advisors during her youth, Joseph Sewall and Samuel Cooper. Sewall was pastor of the famous Old South Church of Boston. Wheatley went to church there until Sewall's death in 1769. About his death she wrote, "I too have a cause this mighty loss to mourn,/For he my monitor will not return."[4] Cooper was the minister of Boston's Brattle Street Meetinghouse. He baptized Wheatley on August 18, 1771.

The poem that made Phillis Wheatley famous had a religious theme. It was about a great English Evangelical preacher who frequently toured New England. "On the Death of the Reverend Mr. George Whitefield" was published in 1770.

From her earliest years, Wheatley was physically frail. In 1773, the Wheatleys gave her freedom and sent her to receive medical care in London. There she met Benjamin Franklin and other notable figures. It was in London that she published *Poems on Various Subjects, Religious and Moral.* Phillis Wheatley was only nineteen years old when the book came out. At the time of its publication, she was the object of vast public attention because she was both a child prodigy and a former slave.

Wheatley had been taken to London partly for reasons of health, but also to meet a number of distinguished persons. Included among them were the Countess of Huntington, the Lord Mayor of

London, and the Earl of Dartmouth. They knew her poetry and wanted to assist her in its publication. When she received word of Susannah Wheatley's fatal illness, Phillis Wheatley returned to Boston sooner than had been planned. If it were not for this, she probably would have been presented to the court of George III.

Wheatley returned to Boston in 1773. The opening shots of the American Revolution were fired near Boston in 1775. She wrote poems in support of the American cause and against British rule. One poem was addressed to George Washington, who had been put in command of the revolutionary armies. Washington wrote to Wheatley and invited her to visit him at the Continental Army camp. The poem she had written for him was reprinted several times as encouragement for the patriot cause.

In 1774, Susannah Wheatley died. Phillis Wheatley married John Peters, a free African American, in 1778. That year, John Wheatley died. Soon Phillis Wheatley's fortunes took a turn for the worse. Her marriage was ill fated. At one point, she worked as a laundress in a lodging house while Peters was in debtor's prison. (He may have been in jail when Phillis Wheatley died.)

The Wheatley family disliked Peters, who moved from job to job. Sidney Kaplan wrote in *The Black Presence in the Era of the American Revolution*, however, that Peters seemed to be a man of dignity. He valued himself and struggled in vain to succeed. He worked as a grocer and was a spokesman for African Americans in the Massachusetts courts. Almost nothing else is known about Wheatley's husband.

Phillis Wheatley spent her last years alone in great poverty in a wreck of a house in Boston. Around 1784, two of her three children died. Her own health quickly declined. Wheatley's third child lay beside her on her deathbed, and died soon after she did. Phillis Wheatley died at about the age of thirty on December 5, 1784. Mother and child were buried together in an unmarked grave.

It would be almost a hundred years before a black writer would write in a different way than whites did. It took that long before African Americans could express their own unique experience. Phillis Wheatley expressed the popular mood of her age. She had a clear sense of poetry and a religious and national spirit.

Wheatley wrote "To S.M., a Young African Painter, on Seeing His Works":

To S.M., a Young African Painter, on Seeing His Works

To show the laboring bosom's deep intent,
And thought in living characters to paint,
when first thy pencil did those beauties give,
And breathing figures learnt from thee to live,
How did those prospects give my soul delight,
A new creation rushing on my sight?
Still, wondrous youth! each noble path pursue,

On deathless glories fix thine ardent view:
Still may the painter's and the poet's fire
To aid thy pencil, and thy verse conspire!
And may the charms of each seraphic theme
Conduct thy footsteps to immortal fame!
High to the blissful wonders of the skies
Elate thy soul, and raise thy wishful eyes.
Thrice happy, when exalted to survey
That splendid city, crowned with endless day,
Whose twice six gates on radiant hinges ring:
Celestial Salem blooms in endless spring.

Calm and serene thy moments glide along,
And may the muse inspire each future song!
Still, with the sweets of contemplation blest,
May peace with balmy wings your soul invest!
But when these shades of time are chased away,
And darkness ends in everlasting day,
On what seraphic pinions shall we move,
And view the landscape in the realms above?
There shall thy tongue in heavenly murmurs flow,
And there my muse with heavenly transport glow:
No more to tell of Damon's tender sighs,
Or rising radiance of Aurora's eyes,
For nobler themes demand a nobler strain,
And purer language on the ethereal plain.
Cease, gentle muse! the solemn gloom of night
Now seals the fair creation from my sight.

Paul Laurence Dunbar

Paul Laurence Dunbar
(1872–1906)

On June 27, 1896, famous novelist William Dean Howells wrote a review of a book by an African-American poet. The essay appeared in *Harper's Weekly*. As a result, an elevator boy who had paid a modest sum to have his first book published was now famous.

A son of former slaves, Paul Laurence Dunbar is widely thought of as the first influential African-American poet. Many critics believe that no African-American "writer of the period had a greater impact."[1] He greeted America with *Lyrics of a Lowly Life* in 1896. The book won him a national reputation, and it enabled him to pursue a literary career for the rest of his life. His acclaim was at first based mainly on poems written in the dialect of plantation folk.

In addition to his verse, Dunbar wrote novels, short stories, essays, and many poems in standard English. His work describes African-American life at the turn of the century. James Weldon Johnson wrote of Dunbar in his *Book of American Negro Poetry*. Johnson said that Dunbar stands out as among the very first African-American writers to be a true master. He called Dunbar the first to earn and keep high honors for what he wrote.[2]

Dunbar wrote about African-American humor, fears, and problems. He felt his race's yearnings, pain, and aspirations. The poet was among the very first notable writers to voice them all.

Born on June 27, 1872, in Dayton, Ohio, Dunbar began to show promise while he was still in high school. He lived in Dayton with his widowed mother, Matilda. His father, Joshua, a former slave, had worked as a soldier and plasterer. His mother was a former slave who worked as a laundress.

The only African American in his high school class, Dunbar became its president and wrote the Central High class poem. By 1889, two years before he graduated, he had already published poems in the *Dayton Herald*. Dunbar also founded and edited the short-lived *Dayton Tattler,* a newspaper for African Americans. The newspaper was printed by Dunbar's classmate, Orville Wright, who with his brother, Wilbur, later gained fame for inventing the airplane.

Although Dunbar aspired to a career in law, his mother's meager income did not allow him to go to college, so he looked for a job with various Dayton businesses, including newspapers. Dunbar was not hired because of his race. He had to settle for work as an elevator operator. When he was not at work, he kept writing.

In 1892, Dunbar was invited by one of his former teachers to address the Western Association of Writers in Dayton. At the meeting, Dunbar made friends with James Newton Matthews, who praised Dunbar's work in a letter to an Illinois newspaper. The letter was reprinted by newspapers throughout the country. Among the readers of this letter was the poet James Whitcomb Riley, who read a lot of Dunbar's work. He wrote a letter commending the young poet. Dunbar was greatly encouraged by the support of both Matthews and Riley, so he decided to publish a collection of his own poems. A Dayton firm then printed *Oak and Ivy* for a small fee.

Dunbar published his earliest African-American dialect poems, as well as many works in standard English, in *Oak and Ivy*. Among the nondialect poems is one of his most popular poems, "Sympathy." This somber poem tells of the dismal plight of his people. In another standard English poem, "Ode to Ethiopia," he records the many great things done by African Americans. He tells his brothers and sisters to maintain their pride despite racial abuse. These and other poems became very popular, which inspired Dunbar to devote himself more fully to writing. While Dunbar wrote many great poems in standard English, he was noted for his dialect pieces. Dialect is a form of speech that is different than the standard for a language. During slavery years, African Americans developed their own dialect.

Many poems were written in the speech of slaves and their free descendants. Dialect writings derived from other cultures, such as those of Europeans who came to America, were also popular. Some African-American dialect poems sound the way many people speak today. Later poets have integrated street talk and the rhythms of soul music and jazz into their verse.

The publication of *Oak and Ivy* made Dunbar and his mother very happy, but it did not relieve their money problems. In 1893, Dunbar left for the Columbian World's Exposition in Chicago. He hoped to find a better job there. He did a number of odd jobs until he met the African-American leader Frederick Douglass, who was commissioner in charge of the Haitian exhibit. Douglass praised Dunbar's poetry. He hired Dunbar as his clerical assistant and paid him five dollars a week out of his own pocket. On Colored Americans Day at the fair, Dunbar sat on the platform with Douglass and other notables before thousands of people. Dunbar read his own poetry before a delighted audience. Douglass inscribed one of his books to Dunbar: "From Frederick Douglass to his dear young poet friend Paul Dunbar, one of the sweetest songsters his race has produced and a man of whom I hope great things."[3]

Shortly after the publication of *Oak and Ivy*, Dunbar was approached by Ohio attorney Charles A. Thatcher, who offered to help finance the poet's college education. Dunbar, inspired by sales of *Oak and Ivy*, turned down Thatcher's offer in order to pursue a literary career. Thatcher then promoted Dunbar in Toledo, Ohio. He arranged for Dunbar to read his poetry at libraries and gatherings. Dunbar also found unexpected support from psychiatrist Henry A. Tobey, who helped him distribute *Oak and Ivy* in Toledo and sent Dunbar money when it was sorely needed.

Tobey and Thatcher eventually published *Majors and Minors*. For this book, Dunbar wrote poems on many themes and in several styles. He grouped the more complex poems, those written in standard English, under the heading "Majors." The African-American dialect works he gathered as "Minors." Dunbar gave most of his energy to his nondialect poetry. He was influenced by the English Romantic poets and Americans such as Riley. His dialect verse earned Dunbar the greatest favor with his mostly white readership, however. These dialect poems gained increasing fame for Dunbar throughout the United States.

Through Thatcher and Tobey, Dunbar met an agent. He was offered more public readings, and he secured a publishing contract. Dunbar then published *Lyrics of a Lowly Life*. The poetry collection was derived primarily from verse already featured in *Oak and Ivy* and *Majors and Minors*. This new volume sold very well across America. Dunbar was now the nation's most famous African-American poet. With this new fame, Dunbar began a six-month reading tour of England, where he found publishers for a British edition of *Lyrics of a Lowly Life*. He also made friends with the composer Samuel Coleridge-Taylor. Dunbar later worked with Coleridge-Taylor in writing the operetta *Dream Lovers*.

When Dunbar returned to the United States in 1897, he obtained a clerkship at the Library of Congress in Washington, D.C. Soon afterward, he married fellow writer Alice Ruth Moore. His health suffered during the two years he lived in Washington, but he continued to write successfully.

Dunbar published his first short story collection in 1898. By the end of that year, his health had become worse. Dunbar then left the Library of Congress and began another reading tour. He published another acclaimed verse collection, *Lyrics of the Hearthside*. Then, in the spring of 1899, he became so ill that he almost died.

Dust from library shelves had collected in Dunbar's lungs and weakened them; he was also ill with pneumonia. Dunbar rested in the mountains but continued to write. In 1900, he published another book of tales, and he went on to write three more novels. His health continued to worsen in the next two years, and he resorted to alcohol to temper his chronic coughing. Dunbar's marriage had always been troubled, and it too became worse due to his reliance on alcohol.

Dunbar and his wife separated in 1902. Unfortunately, the split only contributed to his physical and mental decline. The next year, he suffered a nervous breakdown and another bout of pneumonia. Despite these setbacks, Dunbar managed to publish another book of verse, *Lyrics of Love and Laughter.* The volume describes African-American life in a way that is deep and real. It features both dialect and standard English verse. The book confirmed that he was the country's premier African-American poet.

Dunbar pressed on as a writer despite his illness, until he was too weak to work. He could barely walk for the last two years of his life. By the winter of 1905, he was fatally ill. His lungs and throat were ravaged by tuberculosis. Dunbar died on February 9, 1906, at the age of thirty-three.

During Dunbar's lifetime, he was praised as a great poet who faithfully described African-American people. However, after World War II, he was criticized for writing dialect poetry. Critics complained of his plantation stereotypes. Many of his poems were said to show African Americans in a servile way. Critic Alain Locke said that unlike Dunbar, many poets who came after Dunbar wrote dialect poetry that brought pride to the race. He said these new dialect poets, including Langston Hughes,

Sterling Brown, and Lucy Ariel Williams, used fresh, original language.

Many twentieth-century critics see Dunbar as a tragic victim of his time. They say his talent suffered because he was caught between the demands of publishers and his own desire to free himself from his racial identity. He was seen as being too indirect in praise and protest.

Dunbar's work began to be reevaluated in the late 1960s. The negative critical trend was reversed by the Paul Laurence Dunbar Centenary Celebration at the University of California, Irvine, in 1972. His work was considered in the context of his life, beginning as a nineteen-year-old high school graduate living a shaky life, trying to make a living by his pen, during the Jim Crow Era. The lack of social protest in his work did not mean that he wrote poor poetry. He brought dialect poetry to a new level. He began the literary tradition expressing African-American pride by referring to Ethiopia as "mother," and by celebrating Africa. This was notable because in the 1890s, African history was ignored in America.

Dunbar has been a lasting influence on later African-American poets. Poet Nikki Giovanni hailed Dunbar as a "natural resource" of his people.[4] Dunbar's work is both a history and a celebration of African-American life. *Complete Poems of Paul Laurence Dunbar,* which was published in 1913, has never been out of print. Some of his poems have been used as lyrics for songs that are well known and loved in modern times. Dunbar's poem "Little Brown Baby" is one of his most famous dialect pieces:

Little Brown Baby

Little brown baby wif spa'klin' eyes,
    Come to yo' pappy an' set on his knee.
What you been doin', suh—makin' san' pies?
    Look at dat bib—You's ez du'ty ez me.
Look at dat mouf—dat's merlasses, I bet;
    Come hyeah, Maria, an' wipe off his han's.
Bees gwine to ketch you an' eat you up yit,
    Bein' so sticky an' sweet—goodness lan's!

Little brown baby wif spa'klin' eyes,
    Who's pappy's darlin' an' who's pappy's chile?
Who is it all de day nevah once tries
    Fu' to be cross, er once loses dat smile?
Whah did you git dem teef? My, you's a scamp!
    Whah did dat dimple come f'om in yo' chin?
Pappy do' know you—I b'lieves you's a tramp;
    Mammy, dis hyeah's some ol' straggler got in!

Let's th'ow him outen de do' in de san',
    We do' want stragglers a-layin' 'roun' hyeah;
Let's gin him 'way to de big buggah-man;
    I know he's hidin' erroun' hyeah right neah.
Buggah-man, buggah-man, come in de do',
    Hyeah's a bad boy you kin have fu' to eat.
Mammy an' pappy do' want him no mo',
    Swaller him down f'om his haid to his feet!

Langston Hughes

3

Langston Hughes

(1902–1967)

In February 1941, a Harlem writer was close to a nervous breakdown. He was at the center of a controversy because of a protest poem he had written. Complaints from many sides, illness, and a failed reading tour had made him weary. He was in the hospital, groggy from medicine, when word came that he had been evicted from his apartment. Three subtenants, all of them his friends, had fallen behind on rent at 66 Nicholas Place. Two other friends, his dearest ones, stored his belongings, including many important manuscripts and books, in their basement.

In crisis, he questioned his future. Would he continue to live by his writing, as no African American had ever done? Could he make black

America the main subject of his art? Since whites controlled publishing, could he make them his main audience? Was it a bad idea to try this? Was it just a fantasy?

Many talented black writers emerged in the period known as the Harlem Renaissance. They hoped that great art could change the nation's racist views of African Americans. Among Harlem Renaissance artists, Langston Hughes was the most famous, and he had the longest impact on the American literary scene. The legendary Langston Hughes was the first poet to use the rhythms of black music.

Hughes was born on February 1, 1902, in Joplin, Missouri. His parents were separated. He spent most of his childhood with his maternal grandmother in Lawrence, Kansas. Living with her, he first began to write poetry. His grandmother told him of Lewis Sheridan Leary, her first husband. He had died at Harper's Ferry fighting in John Brown's slave rebellion band. Mary Langston used his sacrifice as a deep moral lesson for her grandson Langston Hughes.

Hughes also lived in Topeka, Kansas, and in Lincoln, Illinois. At fourteen he moved to Cleveland, Ohio, where he stayed with his mother and stepfather.

Hughes spent a few summers in Mexico with his businessman father, who had moved to Mexico to escape American racism. Hughes had a painful relationship with his father from which he never recovered fully. Fortunately, Hughes's mother supported his need to be a poet.

Hughes had begun to write and publish before he brought his vast talent to New York City. He went there to attend Columbia University, which he chose because it was near Harlem. After a year, he left Columbia and he worked on board a merchant ship, sailing to Africa and Europe. While he worked as a cook in a Paris nightclub and as a busboy in Washington, D.C., Hughes also continued to publish poems in New York magazines.

One night at work Hughes found that a famous poet named Vachel Lindsay was in the restaurant. Hughes put some of his poems next to the poet's dinner plate. Lindsay gave a well-attended poetry reading later that night. He read some of Hughes's pieces, too. Newspapers across the country wrote about Lindsay's poetry reading. Hughes became known as a highly talented new African-American poet.

Eleven of Hughes's poems were chosen for an anthology called *The New Negro*, prepared by African-American educator Alain Locke. He drew praise from white supporters of the Harlem Renaissance as well. Langston Hughes became the most recognized poet of the Harlem Renaissance. In 1921, after he published his lyric poem "The Negro Speaks of Rivers," he became known as the "poet laureate of Harlem."

Hughes experimented with his writing. Other

Harlem Renaissance writers such as Jean Toomer and Countee Cullen worked with pure patterns. They wrote traditional poems like those of the English classic poets John Keats and Percy Shelley. Hughes broke free with his writing, and he helped change literature forever. Hughes loved to visit jazz nightclubs in Harlem. He wrote the title poem of *The Weary Blues* to the beat of one of his favorite pianists. He was excited about the new form of poetry he had discovered for himself.

Poems in *The Weary Blues* are warm, exotic, and full of color. Hughes does not rely on form too much. This could be seen as a problem, but with Hughes it is an asset. It gives his verse a sense of freedom, like that in jazz. His poems can sound wise, although they were written by such a young man.

Wealthy white supporters of the Harlem Renaissance helped Hughes until he could support himself. Carl Van Vechten had helped to get *The Weary Blues* published. In 1925, Amy Spingarn, a patron of the arts whom Hughes had met at a party, gave Hughes money for further schooling at Lincoln University. He graduated in 1929.

A woman named Charlotte O. Mason provided grants for his writing in New York City between 1928 and 1930. In 1930, Hughes published a novel, *Not Without Laughter,* that made him very famous. Enough copies were sold that he could now support himself by writing. People began to call him the "bard of Harlem."

In 1931, Hughes won the Harmon Prize. The award is given for achievement in black literature and included a $400 cash prize. Hughes used the money to travel to Cuba and Haiti. On his way home from Haiti, Hughes stopped to do readings at Bethune Cookman College in Daytona Beach, Florida. The president, Mary McCleod Bethune, told him he should tour the South reading his poems. She said thousands of African-American youths would be inspired. He would show them they could amount to something despite the problems their race was facing.

Hughes asked the Rosenwald Fund for a grant to carry out his plan. With part of the $1,000 they sent him, he bought an old car. A former Lincoln classmate taught him to drive and became his business manager. His publisher issued a special one-dollar edition of *The Weary Blues* that Hughes would sell on his tour. Hughes was sure that it would sell and that he would get along financially. Hughes now became a full-time writer. For the rest of his life, "in the words of Arna Bontemps, he [was] a minstrel and a troubadour in the classic sense. He has had no other vocation."[1]

Hughes invented new poetic forms by drawing from blues and jazz. His poems expressed the tough and upbeat times of urban African-American life. His book of poems *Montage of a Dream Deferred,* published in 1951, is the poet's greatest expression of Harlem life. It is also his most successful piece of jazz poetry.

Hughes was also a playwright. With his friend Zora Neale Hurston, he wrote *Mule Bone* in 1930. Hurston collected African-American folklore and wrote popular plays, novels, short stories, and articles. When Hurston copyrighted the work in her name only, their friendship ended.

Another great work came later in Hughes's life. He created a fictional African-American folk speaker, an Everyman, called Jesse B. Semple. Hughes wanted his writing to capture the main oral traditions of his culture.

Jesse B. Semple's last name was meant to sound like "simple." This showed that Jesse is a wise kind of fool. Semple was like the lead character in the 1994 movie *Forrest Gump*. Gump, like Semple, was a plain man who could see through many of life's phony things. The characters of Semple and Gump show that things that seem to be important often are not.

Hughes's "Semple" character first appeared in 1943, in newspapers sketches. For Hughes, the Semple stories were a huge artistic success. They showed that he had a large grasp of both his own culture and many writing styles. Hughes wrote four volumes of Semple sketches.

Hughes chose to write about ordinary people. He once said that his poetry was about "workers, roustabouts, and singers, and job hunters . . . people up today and down tomorrow, working this week and fired the next, beaten and baffled, but determined not to be wholly beaten."[2]

Very few people doubted Hughes's skill as a writer, but at first, some readers wished his portraits of people were more positive. In defense he once wrote, "I knew only the people I had grown up with, and they weren't people whose shoes were always shined, who had been to Harvard, or who had heard of Bach."[3] A large part of his early success was the 1920s hunger for writing that was down-to-earth. Readers found that Hughes's use of blues rhythms satisfied this need.

Hughes's critics sometimes differ in their opinions about his work, but most consider the poems that use blues rhythms to be among his most successful. He wrote excellent short stories in which Semple did not appear, but critics agree that Semple remains Hughes's finest fictional creation.

Hughes edited numerous anthologies, including *An African Treasury,* and *The Best Short Stories by Negro Writers.* With Arna Bontemps, he coedited *The Poetry of the Negro, 1746–1949.* Hughes also published two autobiographies, *The Big Sea* in 1940 and *I Wonder as I Wander* in 1956.

Langston Hughes died on May 22, 1967, in New York City. Writers around the world have cited Langston Hughes's influence on their work. His words appeal to all types of people. Hardly a day goes by when a speaker at a reading, service, or gathering somewhere does not read a work by Langston Hughes. With history as evidence, Hughes will continue to live in hearts and minds for generations to come.

Hughes's poem "Dream Boogie" has music in its words:

Dream Boogie

Good-morning, daddy!
Ain't you heard
The boogie-woogie rumble
Of a dream deferred?

Listen closely:
You'll hear their feet
Beating out and beating out a—

    YOU THINK
    IT'S A HAPPY BEAT?

Listen to it closely:
Ain't you heard
something underneath
like a—

WHAT DID I SAY?

Sure,
I'm happy!
Take it away!

  HEY, POP!
  RE-BOP!
  MOP!

  Y-E-A-H!

Gwendolyn Brooks

Gwendolyn Brooks
(b. 1917)

Gwendolyn Brooks "wrote about being black before being black was beautiful," wrote critic Martha Liebrum.[1] Alice Walker once said that "if there was ever a born poet, I think it is Brooks."[2] Brooks's life and work reflect many changes in African-American culture. The collection of essays, *Say That the River Turns: The Impact of Gwendolyn Brooks* shows the immense love and respect that exists for her. The many African-American artists and writers who contributed to the book wrote of how she has changed poetry in the United States.

Gwendolyn Brooks was born in Topeka, Kansas, on June 7, 1917, to David Anderson and Keziah Corinne (Wims) Brooks. Four weeks later, the family moved to Chicago. Brooks's brother, Raymond, was born sixteen months after his sister. She started writing poetry at the age of seven. By the age of eleven, Brooks was keeping notebooks of poetry. In Chicago, she attended Englewood High School and Wilson Junior College.

The poet had a happy and secure childhood. Her parents were loving and supportive. Brooks's mother was a teacher. Her father, who worked as a janitor, was an intelligent, good-hearted man. He had wanted to be a doctor, and he studied for a year and a half at Fisk University. He read stories to his children and sang songs to them.

Brooks had her share of highs and lows at Englewood High School. The white students did not accept African Americans very well, but Brooks did not try to fit in with these intolerant people. Brooks was reading and learning about newer poets such as T. S. Eliot, e. e. cummings, Ezra Pound, Wallace Stevens, and William Carlos Williams. She was also writing poetry and sending it to famous writers, such as James Weldon Johnson.

At sixteen, she met Langston Hughes. He read her poems right away and gave Brooks enthusiastic encouragement. His enthusiasm greatly inspired the young Brooks. Years later, she and her husband gave Hughes a party in their two-room apartment.

In 1938, two years after her graduation from Woodrow Wilson Junior College, Brooks met her future husband, Henry Lowington Blakely, II. They would marry in 1939, and have two children, Henry and Nora.

During the 1940s and 1950s, Brooks showed vast growth as a poet. She studied the poetry of Pound and Eliot under the guidance of Inez Cunningham Stark, a reader for *Poetry* magazine. During this time, Brooks's mother predicted that her daughter would be "the *lady* Paul Dunbar."[3]

Brooks's poems have raw power and roughness, but her words are not bitter or vengeful. The roughness comes when she shows how hard African-American life can be. Her poems are not angry; they are realistic views of the harsh life in the ghetto.

"Reading Brooks," said Alice Walker, "your whole spiritual past begins to float around in your throat."[4]

In the 1940s, Brooks wrote with the rhythms of the Chicago streets and storefront churches of the ghetto area called Bronzeville. *A Street in Bronzeville* was published in 1945. In it, Brooks used the tones of black Protestant preachers, combining it with street talk, standard English, and American verse. She was seen as being among the best in her focus and technique. Brooks's words painted vivid pictures. They often had strong rhymes and heavy African-American accents.

Brooks also has proved to be a writer who can handle many forms. In addition to her more free-form verse, she uses traditional lyric forms. She has been one of a few modern poets to write many sonnets.

Brooks's poems link two very different generations of African-American poets. In her early work, she had kept the feel of the Harlem Renaissance, whose writers thought people of all races should mix. She had followed the lead of writers like Langston Hughes and Countee Cullen. Her work received most of its support from whites during that time.

In 1967, a huge change happened to Brooks's thoughts about herself, her work, and her world. Until that year, "my own writing did not confront me with a shrill spelling of itself," Brooks has said.[5] At the second Black Writers' Conference at Fisk University, she met many young, new activist poets.

Brooks began to relate to militant groups. She began to define her work as belonging primarily to the African-American community. She did a poetry workshop for the Blackstone Rangers, a teenage gang in Chicago. In a poem called "The Blackstone Rangers," she describes the young, tough, raw members. She contrasts the leaders—Jeff, Gene, Jeronimo and Bop—with Harry Belafonte and Martin Luther King, Jr. Brooks compares them to Stokely Carmichael (Kwame Toure), Malcolm X, and H. Rap Brown. The final section of the poem is about the Rangerettes, the gang girls. Brooks contrasts these sweet and exotic girls with their hard life in the ghetto, and she shows how confusing that life can be.

Brooks has written about African-American inner-city life and hardships, and she also has written superb love poems. "A Lonely Love" describes a secret romance between lovers who can meet only in alleys, hallways, and caverns. The poem's sharp images are combined with religious themes. The work is full of energy.

Brooks published an autobiographical novel, *Maude Martha,* in 1953. The novel follows the life of Maude Martha, a young black woman. Though the novel is fiction, it is based on Brooks's own experiences. Brooks later published a literary autobiography, *Report From Part One,* in 1972. She wrote honestly about the many stages of her career and their place in her life. When she was writing her autobiography, she became conscious of her role as a leader of African-American feminists. Brooks paid special attention to the complex problems of African-American women. In 1996, Brooks completed *Report From Part Two,* which contained the second part of her life story and many new poems.

Brooks has received scores of awards and honors. She was the last Poetry Consultant of the Library of Congress. (The person who holds that post is now known as the Poet Laureate of the United States.) Since 1968, she has been the Poet Laureate of the State of Illinois.

Brooks is the first and only American writer to be chosen for the Society for Literature Award by the University of Thessaloniki in Athens, Greece. She was awarded the Frost Medal, the highest honor of the Poetry Society of America.

The Gwendolyn Brooks Center for Black Literature and Culture opened at Chicago State University in 1993. Brooks is a writer-in-residence at the college. The National Endowment for the Humanities named Brooks its 1994 Jefferson Lecturer. This is one of the federal government's highest honors in the humanities.

Brooks has written about everyday African-American life. She has focused on ordinary people. In 1962 she wrote:

> I think that my poetry is related to life in the broad sense of the word, even though the subject matter relates closest to the Negro. Although I called my first book *A Street in Bronzeville*, I hoped that people would recognize instantly that Negroes are just like other people; they have the same hates and loves and fears, the same tragedies and triumphs and deaths, as people of any race or religion or nationality.[6]

To Gwen with Love, a tribute to Brooks from the community of black writers and artists, shows their love for her. Gwendolyn Brooks has given the world a great gift through her art and her life.

Brooks's poem "To the Diaspora" is addressed to African Americans who did not yet consider themselves beautiful.

To the Diaspora

you did not know you were Afrika
When you set out for Afrika
you did not know you were going.
Because
you did not know you were Afrika.
You did not know the Black continent
that had to be reached
was you.

I could not have told you then that some sun
would come,
somewhere over the road,
would come evoking the diamonds
of you, the Black continent—
somewhere over the road.
You would not have believed my mouth.

When I told you, meeting you somewhere close
to the heat and youth of the road,
liking my loyalty, liking belief,
you smiled and you thanked me but very little believed me.

Here is some sun. Some.
Now off into the places rough to reach.
Though dry, though drowsy, all unwillingly a-wobble,
into the dissonant and dangerous crescendo.
Your work, that was done, to be done to be done to be done.

Amiri Baraka

Amiri Baraka
(b. 1934)

The poet had studied at top universities, and he earned wide fame. In 1966, he returned to hard-pressed Newark, New Jersey, as an African-American activist. He had been born in that city as Everett LeRoi Jones thirty-two years before. He rejected white values after having made a name for himself as LeRoi Jones.

The poet adopted the name Imamu Ameer Baraka. His Africanized name Imamu means "spiritual leader." Ameer means "blessed" and Baraka means "prince." He later shortened it to Amiri Baraka. He became the literary leader of a group of African Americans who proclaimed themselves a separate nation. Baraka was active in politics as well as in literature.

Baraka was born in Newark, on October 7, 1934. He was the son of Coyette Leroy (a postman and elevator operator) and Anna Lois Russ Jones. As a child, Baraka showed ability well beyond his young age. He graduated from high school two years early. He attended Howard University, and spent two and a half years as an aerial climatographer in the U.S. Air Force. Baraka earned a master of arts degree in philosophy at Columbia University. He also studied at Rutgers University and the New School for Social Research, where he earned another master's degree in German literature.

The young writer linked himself with Beat poets, such as Allen Ginsberg. He also joined the circle of poets from the New York school, such as Frank O'Hara. In 1958, with his first wife, Hettie Cohen, who was white, he had started *Yugen* magazine and then the Totem Press. They printed work by poets such as Allen Ginsberg, Jack Kerouac, and Gary Snyder.

At that time, Baraka sought a style that would allow him full and free personal expression of himself. About his work, Baraka said, "'HOW YOU SOUND??' is what we recent fellows are up to. MY POETRY is whatever I think I am."[1] Baraka used new forms of meter and ways of placing words on the page. He wanted to stress the way spoken poetry sounded. Baraka turned to poems that had a strong tone. Charles Olson's work was ideal to project one's voice. Olson based his poetry on the way he himself would read it aloud. Baraka combined these patterns with the rhythms he knew from African-American music, such as the blues.

Baraka's early poems tried to convey a personal anguish. He returns frequently to the problem of a divided self. Part of the pain stemmed from being a black writer in a white world. For the most part, the speakers in his early poems are frozen by fear and guilt.

In "I Substitute for the Dead Lecturer," Baraka speaks of his face being seared by flames, and his black skull and bones being left in an empty cage of failure. Baraka's first two volumes of poetry were *Preface to a Twenty Volume Suicide Note* (1961) and *The Dead Lecturer* (1964). Later in his career, he was to look back at those earlier poems as showing not his problems but a sick society.

In the mid-1960s, Baraka changed his focus through a series of great plays. In these writings, Baraka explored the violent basis of relationships be-tween blacks and whites. His plays *The Toilet, Dutchman,* and *The Slave* treat black-white relation-ships in often shocking ways.

He wrote *Dutchman* in 1964. The story involves an encounter between a young black man and a white woman in a subway. It ends in the murder of the African American. He became well known for the play, which received the *Village Voice*'s Obie Award.

For almost fifteen years, Baraka had tried to use his work to help integrate society. He thought that the literary world, at least, could accept all races. The poet became frustrated in his efforts. After coming to believe such a world was not possible, Baraka said that "the Black Artist's role in America is to aid in the destruction of America as he knows it."[2]

Throughout the 1960s, Baraka became more radical. He rejected white culture and searched for "the dark gods of the black soul." First, he established Black Arts Repertory Theater and School in Harlem in 1965. This school inspired black theaters throughout the country. Then he focused his activities on the politics and social issues facing his race. In 1966, he set up Spirit House, a community center in Newark.

Baraka and his wife, Hettie, divorced in 1965. They had two daughters, Kellie and Lisa. In 1967 Baraka married Sylvia Robinson. The following year, Baraka would drop the name LeRoi Jones and would take his current name. His wife took the name Bibi Amina Baraka. Together, they had five children, Obalaji Malik Ali, Ras Jua Al Aziz, Shani Isis, Amiri Seku, and Ahi Mwenge.

Baraka was involved in the Newark riots in the summer of 1967. He was arrested and charged with carrying a gun. He was tried and found guilty. He was given the most severe sentence ever for his offense. The judge himself admitted that the punishment was based on a racist poem that Baraka published in the *Evergreen Review.*

". . . [Baraka] is very guilty," wrote critic Stephen Schenck, "of something, poetry probably." Schenck added that Baraka was guilty "of speaking in persuasive tongues to the part of the heart that is better left unaroused."[3] Baraka swore that he did not carry guns into the riot and that he had been severely attacked by several policemen. He appealed the stiff sentence and was cleared of carrying a concealed weapon.

In the late sixties, Baraka wrote several volumes of poetry including *Black Art* and *Black Magic: Sabotage; Target Study; Black Art; Collected Poetry.* These encouraged African Americans to create an identity separate from the world of white culture. Baraka's poem "Black Art" announced this view. It expressed that African-American art should be a revolt. In *Black Magic,* poems such as "Sabotage" and "Target" show the poet's militant stance. At the end of "Black Art," the poet says that African Americans want their own poem, and their own world. In "Black Art" Baraka says that all the world should be an African-American poem, and that all his people should speak this poem, in silence or out loud. The piece uses many capital letters. This suggests how strongly his poems had moved toward being read aloud. The works often use the rhythm of chant. They sound right for a rally.

Baraka was the dominant voice of the Black Arts movement. With Larry Neal, Baraka edited the anthology *Black Fire.* The book defined the Black Aesthetic and set the goals of the Black Arts movement. The major goal of the movement was to find new ways of analyzing African-American art in terms of the African-American experience. Other goals came to include defining the African-American art-ist's role in the community and making the arts more meaningful by taking them to the African-American masses.

In 1968, Baraka helped found the Black Community Development and Defense organization. This radical group maintained the belief that blacks and whites should be separate. In 1974, however, Baraka abandoned his black nationalist stance. He called it racist and adopted a philosophy called Third World Socialism. His newer poems then reflected his new Marxist philosophy.

Baraka's story is one of a man transformed. Today, he is a professor of Afro-American Studies at the State University of New York at Stony Brook. He shares his powerful story with students of all races. He still fights for equality.

Amiri Baraka remains a major and controversial writer. His words helped to change the course of African-American art. He celebrates his sisters in the poem "Beautiful Black Women."

Beautiful Black Women . . .

Beautiful black women, fail, they act. Stop them, raining.
They are so beautiful, we want them with us. Stop them,
    raining.
Beautiful, stop raining, they fail. We fail them and their
    lips
stick out perpetually, at our weakness. Raining. Stop
    them. Black
queens, Ruby Dee weeps at the window, raining, being
    lost in her
life, being what we all will be, sentimental bitter frus-
    trated
deprived of her fullest light. Beautiful black women, it is
still raining in this terrible land. We need you. We flex
    our
muscles, turn to stare at our tormentor, we need you.
    Raining.
We need you, reigning, black queen. This/terrible black
    ladies
wander, Ruby Dee weeps, the window, raining, she calls,
    and her voice
is left to hurt us slowly. It hangs against the same wet
    glass, her
sadness and age, and the trip, and the lost heat, and the
    grey cold
buildings of our entrapment. Ladies. Women. We need
    you. We are still
trapped and weak, but we build and grow heavy with
    our knowledge. Women.
Come to us. Help us get back what was always ours.
    Help us, women. Where
are you, women, where, and who, and where, and who,
    and will you help
us, will you open your bodysouls, will you lift me up
    mother, will you
let me help you, daughter, wife/lover, will you

"Beautiful Black Women," used by permission of Amiri Baraka.

Haki R. Madhubuti

6

Haki R. Madhubuti
(b. 1942)

On his own at sixteen, the future poet had two paper routes and worked cleaning a bar. By 1969, at the age of twenty-seven, the young man was a star, making three appearances a week. Across the country, he read and spoke about poetry. About his childhood, he said that "poetry in my home was almost as strange as money."[1] Nonetheless, he went on to become one of the best-known African-American poets.

Today, there are more than 3 million copies of Haki R. Madhubuti's books in print. This makes him one of the best-selling authors of poetry and nonfiction in the world. He has a long list of awards as a writer, publisher, educator, and social activist.

Madhubuti was born Don Lee on February 23,

1942, in Little Rock, Arkansas. He was the son of Jimmy L. and Maxine Graves Lee. In 1943, they migrated to Michigan. Madhubuti's sister, Jacqueline, is a year and a half younger than he. They grew up on the Lower East Side of Detroit.

The 1940s and 1950s were harsh times for Madhubuti and his family. His father wandered in and out of their lives from the day they hit Detroit. Alone and unskilled, his mother ended up working as a janitor. Maxine Lee cleaned a three-story building owned by an African-American preacher/ undertaker. Madhubuti's earliest memory is of his mother's hard work there. Once a week, she carried garbage cans on her back to the alley. It was rare for Madhubuti to see his mother without a washcloth, mop, or broom in her hands.

At this time, Madhubuti was eight years old and his sister was seven. They helped their mother as much as possible. They knew that in order to stay in their apartment, they had to keep the building clean. What they did not know was that staying there also depended upon their mother's having sex with the building owner. They stayed in the apartment until their mother was able to find work that at first seemed to be less taxing on her mind and body.

Maxine Lee next worked as a barmaid, serving drinks at Sonny Wilson's, a popular bar in Detroit. At this job, she started to consume large amounts of alcohol. By the time Madhubuti was thirteen, his mother was a confirmed alcoholic. By the time he was fifteen, his mother had moved on to hard drugs and could not function most of the time.

Next, Madhubuti's sister, who had just turned fourteen, announced that she was pregnant. Madhubuti went looking for the man who had impregnated her, a twenty-one-year-old local gang leader, with little potential as a husband or father. A fight ensued, and Madhubuti was brutally beaten. When he went home, his mother gave Madhubuti another whipping for getting whipped.

Maxine Lee's need for drugs and alcohol increased. She began to prostitute herself to get money to feed her habit. Madhubuti spent many nights searching for her in Detroit's cheap hotels. Just before he turned sixteen, his mother overdosed on drugs and died. His sister was pregnant again. Before she was thirty, she had six children and had never been married.

What saved him? When he was thirteen, Madhubuti's mother asked him to go to the public library and check out *Black Boy* by Richard Wright. "I refused to go because I didn't want to go anywhere and ask for anything black," Madhubuti said. "The self hatred that occupied my mind, body and soul simply prohibited me from going to a white library in 1955 to request from a white librarian a book by a black author, especially with Black in the title."[2]

Madhubuti has said that no one ever told him directly that he should hate himself. He was the product of an education that taught children to read and respect the achievements of white Americans only. Madhubuti believes that America sometimes subtly, and quite often openly, taught him white supremacy. He learned to hate himself.[3] When Madhubuti saw how important *Black Boy* was in his mother's mind, he finally went to the library and read the book that would deeply change his life.

Madhubuti found the life of Richard Wright to be just like his own. He also noticed that Wright's words about African Americans were not insulting. Madhubuti began to read other works by African-American authors.

After his mother's death, Madhubuti moved to Chicago. He was sixteen. He stayed with an aunt for a while, then rented a room at the Southside YMCA. Madhubuti completed high school in Chicago and ended up in St. Louis, Missouri, where he joined the United States Army in 1961.

When he arrived at boot camp, he was one of three African Americans among 197 white men. As Madhubuti stepped off the bus, the drill sergeant noticed a copy of Paul Robeson's *Here I Stand* in Madhubuti's hand. (Paul Robeson was one of the greatest African-American leaders, athletes, performers, and scholars of the twentieth century.) The sergeant made a racist remark and tore the pages from the book. He gave one to each recruit and ordered them to use the pages as toilet paper.

Madhubuti's reading about African Americans

had given him the strength to deal with this trauma. At that time, Madhubuti decided never again to apologize for being African American. He would reeducate himself.

Madhubuti became a sponge for reading. It was as important to him as water or food. He chose to seek information about the world around him. The sergeant's reaction to his book had taught Madhubuti the power of ideas. He decided to get into the business of ideas, to change the world for the better. During his two years in the military, Madhubuti read almost a book a day. When he left the army in August 1963, his goal was to serve the great majority of his people. Madhubuti wanted to provide a voice to those without one, so in 1967, he founded the Third World Press in Chicago. Although he began the company with two friends and a mimeograph machine, it is now one of the largest African-American publishers in the world. Madhubuti also sought to provide education to African Americans, so he started the Institute of Positive Education/New Concept Development Center in 1969.

Madhubuti was inspired to become a poet by African-American music, lifestyle, churches, and people. His poetry presents the beauty and joy of the African-American experience. At the same time, his poems express outrage at the oppression of his people. They reflect raw courage. Madhubuti's style makes his "lines rumble like a street gang on the page," wrote critic Liz Gant.[4] His collections include *Don't Cry, Scream* and *We Walk the Way of the New World.* Like a composer of music, Madhubuti wants his poems to be performed. His words are designed to convey an African-American speaking voice. Often using street talk, Madhubuti draws his audience to participate. He stresses unity for his people.

Madhubuti's strong words are not just a protest; they inspire people to act. His critics have said that his work shows hatred, but Gwendolyn Brooks defended him in the introduction to *Don't Cry, Scream.* She said that Madhubuti writes for and to African Americans. "The last thing these people crave is elegance," she wrote. "It is very hard to enchant, with elegant song, the ears of a fellow whose stomach is growling."[5]

Scholar Steven Henderson, in praising Madhubuti, said that he is more widely imitated than any other African-American poet except Amiri Baraka. Madhubuti is one of the most important writers of the Black Arts movement.

At the height of the Black Arts movement, new writers turned not to mainstream publications but to African-American ones. African Americans produced a burst of poetry. Like Madhubuti, they often used elements of pop culture and African-American dialect in their poems.

In addition to Larry Neal and Amiri Baraka, poets including Madhubuti and Sonia Sanchez were often published in journals such as *The Journal of*

Black Poetry and *Negro Digest* (later renamed *Black World* and then *First World*), *Black Dialogue, Soulbrook, Freedomways, Umbra,* and *Liberator.* New African-American voices were welcomed and established. Madhubuti was a key figure who helped to define the issues to be debated: What was the nature and function of African-American literature? How did it relate to the political struggle for Black Power? How useful was the writing? Exactly how was it to be useful?

Some African-American writers thought that African-American literature should be judged by its contribution to the condition of African Americans living in the United States. Others thought that the Black Aesthetic should reject the theories and methods used by whites to criticize black literature.

Madhubuti lives in Chicago with his wife, Safisha. He has five children: Mariama, Don Patrick, Laini, Bomani, and Akili. He is currently a professor of English at Chicago State University. He is also director of Chicago State's Gwendolyn Brooks Center.

Madhubuti has received many honors. Among his many awards are the American Book Award, the Black Caucus Award of the National Council of Teachers of English, and honors from the African American Cultural Center of Los Angeles Foundation.

Madhubuti is one of the founders of the Organization of Black American Culture Writers'

Workshop. He is also a founder and board member of the National Association of Black Book Publishers.

Madhubuti's influence is still growing. He is a regular writer and editor for many magazines, quarterlies, and newspapers. The poet has also appeared on several television and radio shows.

Madhubuti's stirring poem "Assassination" is about a tragic event in history.

Assassination

it was wild.
the
bullet hit high.
                    (the throat-neck)
& from everywhere:
            the motel, from under bushes and cars,
            from around corners and across streets,
            out of the garbage cans and from rat holes
            in the earth
they came running.
with
guns
drawn
they came running
toward the King—
                    all of them
                    fast and sure—
as if
the King
was going to fire back.
they came running,
fast and sure,
in the
wrong
direction.

"Assassination" by Haki R. Madhubuti. Copyright © 1969 from his
book *Don't Cry, Scream*, published by Third World Press, Chicago.

Nikki Giovanni

Nikki Giovanni

(b. 1943)

Nikki Giovanni roared out of the Black Arts movement of the 1960s. She is one of the most widely read of our living poets. Despite progress, racism is still our national shame, and Nikki Giovanni is as fiercely committed as ever to the fight for equality: "I believe that if I keep examining my life and what I think and feel, I will have added one teeny, tiny bit of truth to this planet I call home."[1]

> I am a poet. Poets are not special people, we only function in a special profession. So do doctors or lawyers or teachers or most people. We are not different; what we do is different. Once we understand that variations of birth as to country, race, gender, and age are just that—different.[2]

Giovanni established herself as one of the preeminent figures in the African-American literary renaissance of the 1960s. She has achieved international acclaim as a poet, essayist, and lecturer. Giovanni's speaking tours in the United States and Europe have earned her the title "Princess of Black Poetry" because her readings often attract large, enthusiastic crowds. The poet is best known for her books of poems on the themes of self-discovery and black consciousness. Giovanni also has received praise from critics for her several volumes of children's verse. Her recordings of poetry read to music are adored. They include the best-selling *Truth is on Its Way.*

Yolande Cornelia Giovanni, Jr., was born on June 7, 1943, in Knoxville, Tennessee. She was the second child of Yolande and Jones "Gus" Giovanni. The poet was the younger daughter in a close-knit family. The family moved to Cincinnati, Ohio, in August 1943. She still considers the city home. Giovanni was very close to her sister, Gary, and to her maternal grandmother, Luvenia Terrell Watson. Watson taught Giovanni responsibility to her own race. In 1957, Giovanni moved to Knoxville to live with her grandparents. She attended Austin High School.

Giovanni's grandparents were an important influence in her life and on her work. Her very strong-minded maternal grandmother was extremely intolerant of white people. Her husband, John

"Book" Watson, had to smuggle her and other family members out of Albany, Georgia, because Luvenia's outspokenness had given them reason to believe that her life was in danger. They had hoped to reach the north, but settled in Knoxville, the first town that they found to be large enough for them. Book Watson, a teacher, returned to Albany to finish the school term. He then returned to Knoxville, to the family's new home.[3]

The poet's parents and her older sister, Gary, were strong, positive influences. Giovanni's mother, Yolande Watson, was the oldest of three daughters. Yolande met Jones Giovanni at Knoxville College. They married and had two daughters. Jones's roots were in Cincinnati, where Giovanni spent some of her growing-up years. Speaking of her last name, Giovanni said, "It just means that our slave masters were Italian instead of English or French."[4]

Giovanni enrolled in Fisk University, in Nashville, Tennessee, in 1960. She had come from her middle-class family having read a great deal. The young poet, who was in a stage of personal growth and change, came into conflict with Fisk's dean of women. Giovanni went home for Thanksgiving without asking the dean's permission because of her belief that family comes first. Because of her action, Giovanni was "released" from school. She returned home, worked at a drugstore, and took occasional classes at the University of Cincinnati. In 1964, she returned to Fisk and became a serious student.

She also became a budding African-American civil rights activist. One of her first achievements on campus was organizing a successful demonstration to restore the Fisk chapter of the Student Nonviolent Coordinating Committee (SNCC). The group had lost its charter. SNCC was a leading organization in the fight for Civil Rights in the 1960s.

The poet received her bachelor of arts degree in 1967. That year she also organized the first Cincinnati Black Arts Festival. The next year, Giovanni attended the funeral of Martin Luther King, Jr. She was determined to fight for equality with her writing and her life. She received a grant from the National Foundation of the Arts to attend Columbia University's School of Fine Arts, and she moved to New York City.

Giovanni published two books of poetry in 1968 and 1970, *Black Feeling, Black Talk,* and *Black Judgement.* The poems in these volumes cover many aspects of Giovanni's life at that time, including her commitment to a revolution of the oppressed. Giovanni's vision of revolution goes beyond violent change to a vision of rebuilding. The poet is not urging violence in this poetry, but demanding black assertiveness. She was also angry at society's reaction to revolutionary leaders. Some of her poetry was about her lovers and her romantic feelings for them. Finally, she wrote about her family and her emotionally secure childhood.

The poems in these books immerse the reader in

the African-American spirit. They reject negative ways of thinking. They are directed at other African Americans whom she wanted to awaken to the beauty of being African American. They are also directed at herself.

Giovanni's earliest works were enormously successful. *Black Judgement* sold six thousand copies in three months, selling five to six times more than the average book of poetry. Giovanni's poems of the period brought her prominence as one of the leading figures of the new African-American poetry between 1968 and 1971. Speaking engagements began to fill much of her time. In 1970, she edited and published *Night Comes Softly,* an anthology of poetry by black women.

Giovanni's work through the mid-1970s reflects a change in focus. She wrote a collection of autobiographical essays, *Gemini,* and two books of adult poetry, *My House* and *The Women and the Men.* These works show the personal, soul-searching side of Giovanni. The words allow portions of herself and her views to blossom. These parts of Giovanni were seen only in fragments in her earlier works. The writing shows that her creative and moral powers grew sharper. Her understanding of politics and her focus on society deepened. The revolution fades from the new poems; in its place is a growing sense of frustration. Giovanni also shows a greater concern with the nature of poetry itself.

The core of Giovanni's work always relates to

her family: the family that produced her and the family she is producing. Giovanni gave birth to a son, Thomas Watson Giovanni, on August 31, 1969. The poet believes that a good family spirit is what produces healthy communities. This should produce a strong African-American nation.[5]

Along with her poetry for adults, Giovanni has published several volumes of poetry for children, including *Spin a Soft Black Song, Ego-Tripping and Other Poems for Young People,* and *Vacation Time.* Giovanni's poems combine casual energy and sudden wit. Her children's poems, like Giovanni's adult poetry, are concerned with racial pride and individual love. The poet explores childhood with honest affection. Many of Giovanni's works use the rhythms of African-American music. In her singing lines, Giovanni shows that she hasn't forgotten her childhood adventures. She explores the world with a small person's sense of discovery.

As early as 1971, Giovanni began using another medium for presenting her poetry—sound recording. *Truth is on Its Way* was the best-selling spoken-word album of the year. The popularity of *Truth is on Its Way* encouraged Giovanni to make many other recordings of her poetry. She also made audio- and videotapes with other poets about poetry and African-American issues.

In 1978, Giovanni published *Cotton Candy on a Rainy Day,* which is perhaps her most sobering book of verse. It contains thoughtful poems about the feelings, fears, realities, and responsibilities of living. The book also mourns the loss of the hope that came when the 1960s ended.

Some of Giovanni's more recent work includes another collection of poems, *Those Who Rode the Night Winds,* in 1983, and *Sacred Cows and Other Edibles* in 1988. In 1994, she published a collection of essays called *Racism 101,* which continues her fight for equality. Giovanni published a number of books in 1996, including two books of poetry for children, and a collection of her works, *The Selected Poems of Nikki Giovanni.*

Throughout her career, Giovanni has been given numerous honors. Several universities have awarded her honorary doctorate degrees including her alma mater, Fisk University. She was named Woman of the Year by Ebony magazine in 1970 and by Mademoiselle in 1971. The McDonald's Literary Achievement Award for poetry was established in Giovanni's name in 1988.

Today, Nikki Giovanni is a professor of English at Virginia Polytechnic Institute and State University in Blacksburg, Virginia, where she teaches creative writing. She is still in demand around the world as a speaker.

In the course of twenty years, Giovanni's work has evolved. It started as open, aggressive, and explosive verse. She fought for a revolution, using words. Later works expressed sensitivity, beauty, tenderness, warmth, and depth. Nonetheless, a central theme runs through all of Giovanni's poetry. Giovanni has a deep concern about her identity. She cares about what her purpose in life should be. When the poet looks inside herself in this way, she often blends these concerns with her social and political activism. Giovanni writes out of her own experiences, which also happen to be the experiences of her people. As an artist, she shows what she sees.

Giovanni's poem "Knoxville, Tennessee" is both gentle and full of energy.

knoxville, tennessee

I always like summer
best
you can eat fresh corn
from daddy's garden
and okra
and greens
and cabbage
and lots of
barbecue
and buttermilk
and homemade ice-cream
at the church picnic
and listen to
gospel music
outside
at the church
homecoming
and go to the mountains with
your grandmother
and go barefooted
and be warm
all the time
not only when you go to bed
and sleep

Maya Angelou

Maya Angelou

(b. 1928)

It was a historic day in January 1993. President Bill Clinton stared at the poised poet. The sun shone brightly over the capitol. The crowd beyond the stage stood in awed silence. They listened to the poet's smooth, strong voice. Clinton himself had selected this icon of women's strength to read at his inauguration ceremonies. With her inaugural poem "On the Pulse of Morning," the writer touched the hearts and minds of America.

Maya Angelou's life is her poem. Her great talents span many fields. She is best known as the author of *I Know Why the Caged Bird Sings*. Published in 1970, it is the first volume of her five-part autobiography. In this book, she recalls her childhood years. The work was the subject of a two-hour CBS television special in 1979.

Born Marguerite Johnson on April 4, 1928, Angelou overcame the hardships of her youth. Her story is as powerful and complex as the woman herself. She was born in St. Louis, where her worldly, glamorous mother lived. Maya's parents, Vivian Baxter and Bailey Johnson, were separated at the time, so she and her brother Bailey, Jr. were raised in Stamps, Arkansas, by their maternal grandmother, who ran a general store.

At the age of eight Angelou was sent back to live with her mother in California. There she was raped by her mother's boyfriend, Mr. Freeman. When Mr. Freeman was kicked to death, Angelou felt as if his murder was her fault. She entered a self-imposed world of silence that lasted five years. Angelou was sent back to live with her grandmother in Stamps. There, a neighbor, Bertha Flowers, helped draw Maya out of her silence. Flowers gave Angelou books of poetry and discussed them with her. She urged her to recite poems. Angelou also began writing poetry.

Another test came at age sixteen, when Angelou became the unwed mother of a son, Guy. She later described him as "the best thing that ever happened to me."[1] By the time she was in her early twenties, Angelou had also been a Creole cook, a streetcar conductor, a cocktail waitress, a dancer, and a madam.

When she was twenty-two, Angelou married a white man, a former sailor named Tosh Angelos.

She was trying to bring some order to her life. The two-and-a-half-year marriage failed because of her need for freedom in her daily life.

In the following decades, Angelou emerged as an American hero. She has been a dancer, singer, actress, poet, playwright, magazine writer and editor, scriptwriter, television writer and producer, lecturer and civil rights leader.

In 1952, she earned a scholarship to study dance with Pearl Primus in New York. She then joined a twenty-two-country State Department–sponsored European and African tour of George Gershwin's opera *Porgy and Bess.* The opera is about life on the Charleston, South Carolina, waterfront.

Around this time, Angelou took on her present name. Maya was her brother Bailey's nickname for her, and Angelou was a variation of her husband's surname, Angelos.

When Angelou returned from her tour, she became involved in the African-American civil rights movement. Working with Godfrey Cambridge, she produced, directed, and starred in *Cabaret for Freedom* at the Village Gate in New York City in 1960. The show raised money for the Southern Christian Leadership Conference (SCLC), the civil rights group headed by Dr. Martin Luther King, Jr. Later, Dr. King would ask Angelou to become the northern coordinator for the SCLC.

Angelou married Vasumzi Make, a South African freedom fighter in 1960. They moved with

Angelou's son Guy to Africa in 1961. In Cairo, Egypt, she began writing for a newspaper. She became the first woman editor of the *Arab Observer* (Cairo), the only English-language newsweekly in the Middle East. Angelou's marriage soured, and in 1962, she moved to Ghana. There she was the feature editor of the *African Review*. In 1965, she returned to the United States.

Angelou began producing books after some notable friends, including the novelist James Baldwin, heard Angelou's stories of her childhood. "Growing up is painful for the Southern Black girl," writes Maya Angelou in her introduction to *I Know Why the Caged Bird Sings*.[2]

Despite her disadvantages, *I Know Why the Caged Bird Sings* is a joyful account of Angelou's early life. The book tells her story up to age sixteen and it ends with the birth of her son, Guy. The book was praised by critics and sold in high volume. Many of the stories in the book are grim, but the author finds joy by showing the awakening of her young self. Critic M.F.K. Fisher called Angelou's work "true poetry." She said that "it is astounding, flabbergasting to recognize it, in all the words I read every day and night. . . . It gives me heart, to hear so clearly the caged bird singing and to understand her notes, at least a little."[3]

Angelou is hailed as one of the great voices among writers today. Among her many books are eight collections of poetry, including *Just Give Me a*

Cool Drink of Water 'Fore I Diiie, Oh Pray My Wings Are Gonna Fit Me Well, And Still I Rise, Shaker, Why Don't You Sing?, and *Complete Collected Poems of Maya Angelou.* GWP Records recorded *The Poetry of Maya Angelou* in 1969. Angelou published *Phenomenal Woman,* a collection of four long poems celebrating women, in 1995.

Speaking of Angelou's verse, legendary African-American writer James Baldwin wrote, "You will hear regal woman; the mischievous street girl; you will hear the price of a black woman's survival and you will hear generosity. . . . Black, bitter, and beautiful, she speaks of our survival. People can only survive by facing themselves and each other. Sister Maya has been there and back. She knows something about herself and she knows something about us."[4]

Angelou shines light on the African-American woman's intense life and love in *Just Give Me a Cool Drink of Water 'Fore I Diiie.* She has been called one of the world's most exciting women. Her honest poems express the pain of being a woman. *Just Give Me a Cool Drink of Water 'Fore I Diiie* was nominated for a Pulitzer Prize in 1972.

Angelou wrote and produced a ten-part television series on African traditions in American life for National Education Television. She was the original screenwriter and composer for the film *Georgia,* the first original script by a black woman to be produced. She has composed many musical scores for her own films and others.

Angelou has worked for Oprah Winfrey's Harpo Productions, for which she wrote a segment of the television series *Brewster Place*. She won an Emmy nomination for her role in the television series *Roots*. Angelou has been author and executive producer of several television specials herself, including a 1988 BBC-TV documentary called *Trying to Make It Home*. Her poetry was featured in John Singleton's box-office hit *Poetic Justice*.

Angelou has been awarded more than thirty honorary doctorate degrees. She has a long list of awards for her accomplishments and her continued service to the cause of civil rights. In 1981 Angelou received a lifetime appointment as Reynolds Professor of American Studies at Wake Forest University in Winston-Salem, North Carolina.

Angelou's genius lies in the way she uses language to describe her life. Her words evoke vivid images. In her autobiography, the author chooses to re-create the past and to accept it, in both its pretty and its ugly aspects. Angelou tells people to accept themselves, whether they are strong or weak.

This strong sense of self comes out when Angelou reads aloud. The poet is a master before audiences; her stage presence is electrifying. Angelou dresses in bright colors and stands with the strength of a statue. She often wears clothing of African design. The woman moves with energy. Her vigor flows with the rhythm of the lines. Her body language gives life to the tone and meaning of the words. Her life is her poem onstage; Angelou and the poem become one.

Angelou shows her softer romantic side in "Late October."

Late October

Carefully
the leaves of autumn
sprinkle down the tinny
sound of little dyings
and skies sated
of ruddy sunsets
of roseate dawns
roil ceaselessly in
cobweb greys and turn
to black
for comfort.

Only lovers
see the fall
a signal end to endings
a gruffish gesture alerting
those who will not be alarmed
that we begin to stop
in order simply
to begin
again.

Eloise Greenfield

Eloise Greenfield
(b. 1929)

The girl dreaded writing in school. She did not have a problem with grammar and spelling; she didn't like to write because she was shy. She didn't want to put thoughts and feelings on paper. She loved words, but she loved to read them, not write them. The girl loved their sounds and rhythms. She even liked odd things, like homonyms and silent letters.

Eloise Greenfield believes that during those early years, her writing was being stored.[1] She also grew fond of books and movies. She was building up knowledge and feelings. The sounds, rhythms, and meanings of words were creating a great future writer.

Greenfield has written several popular books of verse, including *Honey I Love, Under the Sunday*

Tree, and *Nathaniel Talking.* Her work is shared and loved in schools and homes across the country. The recording of *Honey I Love* has been widely praised by critics. The book was twice named a Notable Book by the American Library Association. Greenfield's first book of poetry, *Honey I Love,* is the most popular of all her books. Young people strongly relate to her poetry.

Greenfield was born in Parmele, North Carolina, on May 17, 1929. The Great Depression had just begun. She grew up during its worst years. When she was four months old, her family moved to Washington, D.C. Her father, Weston Little, had gone ahead a month earlier, looking for work. Once he found a job, he sent for Greenfield, her mother, Lessie, and her brother, Weston, Jr. She has lived there ever since. "Though money was far from plentiful, we managed," Greenfield said. "Family, neighbors and friends made it an enjoyable time."[2] After moving to Washington, the Little's had three other children, a boy, Gerald, and two girls, Vedie and Vera.

Washington, D.C., was segregated when she grew up. The poet faced racist treatment on a regular basis. Her parents explained that the rude people were ignorant. Facing unfair treatment as an African American has given Greenfield a serious commitment to bettering her community. On her way to becoming a great poet and prose writer, she attended Miner Teacher's College. Greenfield describes how she educated herself in poor surroundings:

Until I was 14, there was no library within close walking distance of our house, so every few weeks my father would take us in the car to the nearest one to get a supply of books. Finally, though, a branch of the public library was opened in the basement of a nearby apartment building. For the next few years, I practically lived there, and I worked there part-time during the two years that I was in college.[3]

Music was and still is important in her life. Greenfield took piano lessons and sang in her school's glee club. Early in life, her only goal was to be the teacher in charge of plays and singing. Greenfield forgot about that as she grew up. In her early twenties, she began to search for satisfying work; she later found it in writing. Writing combined her joy in sounds and rhythms with her interest in stories and words. In a 1975 speech to the International Reading Association, she spoke of this connection:

If you love home and you love music and you love words, the miracle is that the poet chose those words and put them together in that order, and it is something to shout about. I [feel] like the Southern Black preachers who, in reciting from the Scriptures, would suddenly be surprised by an old, familiar phrase and would repeat it over to savor and to celebrate this miracle of words.[4]

In the 1960s, Greenfield held a full-time Civil Service job. Her husband, Robert Greenfield, was a procurement specialist for the U.S. Navy. Attention to him and to their children, Monica and Steven, was her priority. Gradually, Greenfield came to believe that there were far too few books that told the truth about African Americans. She wanted to change that. "I don't remember what actually started me, but the first thing I wrote was a rhyme," Greenfield said. "I remember writing different rhymes I thought were funny; I don't know if my family thought they were or not, but they were required to laugh at them."[5] She was bored with her government job as a clerk-typist. She had been doing it since she left school, but Greenfield did not want that job for the rest of her life.

Greenfield decided to write three stories. If none of them sold, she would give up writing and try something else. After she received three rejection slips, she decided she had no writing talent. Over the next several years, however, she read and spoke with many people about writing. Greenfield first wrote in solitude; she nervously avoided discussing her work with other writers. Then she began to believe that talent must have direction. Greenfield pored over books about the craft. She sought the ideas of other writers. She thought she needed a knowledge of techniques in order to use her talent.

Greenfield's first publication was a poem that appeared on the editorial page of the *Hartford Times*. She then began to publish stories in the *Negro Digest*, which later became *Black World*. Greenfield wrote one or two stories a year until she began writing for children. Now an influential writer, she also has contributed to *Ebony Jr.!, Ms., The Horn Book Magazine,* and *Interracial Books for Children Bulletin.*

Greenfield has produced an extensive body of work. In addition to poetry, she has written picture books, biographies, essays, and novels. Her work has received many prestigious honors and awards, including the 1990 Recognition of Merit Award presented by the George C. Stone Center for Children's Books in Claremont, California. Many organizations have officially praised Greenfield as a writer. They include the Council on Interracial Books for Children, the District of Columbia Association of School Librarians, and Celebrations in Learning. Her biography *Rosa Parks* won the Carter G. Woodson Award. *Paul Robeson* won the Jane Addams Children's Book Award. Three picture books received major citations: *She Come Bringing Me That Little Baby Girl* won the Irma Simonton Black Award, *Africa Dream* won the Coretta Scott King Award, and *Me and Nessie* was an American Library Association Notable Book.

Greenfield's collections of poetry include the critically acclaimed classic *Nathaniel Talking.* The poems in this book celebrate the life of an African-American boy who shows deep, gentle, and joyful feelings to which all children can relate. Some of her other books of verse are *Under the Sunday Tree* and *Night on a Neighborhood Street.*

Greenfield has often found time to work with other writers. She headed the Adult Fiction and Children's Literature divisions of the Washington, D.C., Black Writer's Workshop. The group, which no longer exists, encouraged the writing and publishing of African-American literature. She does most of her workshops in the D.C. area, but she also travels. Greenfield has given free workshops on the writing of African-American literature for children.

Greenfield is now a member of the African American Writers Guild. She has used grants from the Washington, D.C., Commission on the Arts and Humanities to teach creative writing to elementary and junior high students. Greenfield believes that the value of a book comes from its application. She has audiotaped her works for the blind, and she visits schools regularly. Greenfield told the *Washington Post* that "seeing the reaction to the words and the realism and respect that you have touched makes you feel like continuing. . . ."[6]

Greenfield has also said, "When I'm carrying a story around in my head, I feel as if I'm holding my head funny. . . . Sometimes I want to explain to people on the street that I'm just trying to keep the words from spilling out until I get a quiet place with pen and paper."[7]

Greenfield is as bright and energetic today as she always has been. The world of children's literature can look forward to her dynamic presence for years to come. Her love for people, truth, and the African-American community are a great gift to us all. "Way Down in the Music" is one of Greenfield's classic poems.

Way Down in the Music

I get way down in the music
Down inside the music
I let it wake me
            take me
Spin me around and make me
Uh-get down

Inside the sound of the Jackson Five
Into the tune of Earth, Wind and Fire
Down in the bass where the beat comes from
Down in the horn and down in the drum
I get down
I get down

I get way down in the music
Down inside the music
I let it wake me
            take me
Spin me around and shake me
I get down, down
I get down

"Way Down in the Music," from *Honey, I Love*, HarperCollins Publishers. Text © 1978 by Eloise Greenfield. Reprinted by permission.

Rita Dove

Rita Dove

(b. 1952)

A little girl in Akron, Ohio, entitled her first poem "The Rabbit With the Droopy Ear." She began writing the poem with no idea how Mr. Rabbit was going to fix his ear. The young poet kept writing; the sad rabbit went to the wise old owl, who gave the rabbit a cure. He told Mr. Rabbit to hang upside down from a tree. Now the rabbit was happy, for both ears were hanging up. The poem itself had told the poet the answer. She learned that she could tell a story with a poem.

In 1993, the librarian of Congress, James H. Billington, appointed Rita Dove to the position of United States Poet Laureate. Along with it came the duties of Consultant in Poetry at the Library of Congress. Dove was the first African American to receive this honor; she was also the youngest. Poet Laureate is the highest official American literary honor.

In 1994, Dove's appointment as Poet Laureate of the United States was renewed for a second year. (A two-year term is the maximum allowed by law.) Dove is well known for her book of poems *Thomas and Beulah*. In 1987, the collection won her a Pulitzer Prize. This made her the second African-American poet (after Gwendolyn Brooks) to receive the award.

Dove was born in Akron, Ohio, on August 28, 1952. Her parents were Ray and Elvira Dove. They were the first in their working-class families to earn advanced degrees. Her father was one of the first African-American research chemists. In the 1950s, he broke the race barrier in the rubber industry. Akron is a town that is known for its rubber factories. Dove and her siblings (two younger sisters, Robin and Rhonda, and one older brother, Ray) grew up in a loving but strict home. "We knew we were expected to carry 'the prize,' the respect that had been earned, a little further down the line. We had to do our best at all times. There were no excuses."[1]

Dove's national acclaim began early in her life. She quickly established a great academic reputation. In 1970, Dove was invited to the White House as a Presidential Scholar, she was one of the two best high school graduates in Ohio. Dove was also one of the one hundred most outstanding high school graduates in the country.

In her autobiography, Dove said that she was raised to be proud of her heritage. Her parents told her about the evils of racism. "They also conveyed the impression that times were changing, and our abilities would be recognized."[2] They stressed the importance of education:

> Education was the key: That much we knew, and so I was a good student. I brought home straight A's on my report card and hoarded the shiny dimes I got for each of them. Which is not to say I didn't like school—I adored learning new things and looked forward to what intellectual adventures each school day would bring; some of the luckiest magic was to open a book and to come away from it wiser after having been lost in its pages.[3]

As a National Achievement Scholar, Dove attended Miami University in Oxford, Ohio. She graduated summa cum laude with a degree in English. In 1973, Dove received a prestigious Fulbright/Hays fellowship to study modern European literature at Tübingen University in Germany. She also had a grant from the International Working Period for Authors Fellowship for West Germany. Dove earned a master of fine arts degree at the University of Iowa in 1977. While she was a graduate student, Dove met her future husband, the German writer Fred Viebahn. Their daughter, Aviva, was born in 1983.

Dove's first poetry collection was called *The Yellow House on the Corner.* Its intense poems are about adolescence. The book was published in 1980 by Carnegie-Mellon University Press. By then, appearances in national magazines and anthologies had already won Dove wide acclaim. While on fellowship in Europe, Dove began her second book, *The Museum.* Her distance from home allowed her to look at many of her own experiences in America. The separation allowed her to imagine many different lives. In *The Museum,* Dove dramatically extended the range of her poetry. Dove has also published a book of short stories as well as poetry collections, including *Grace Notes* and *The Other Side of the House.*

Thomas and Beulah loosely tells the story of her grandparents' lives. The poems are an extended sequence. "It's not a dramatic story—absolutely nothing tragic happened in my grandparents' life," Dove said. "But I think these are people who are often ignored and lost."[4] Dove described the origins of the book this way: My grandmother had told me a story that had happened to my grandfather when he was young, coming up on a riverboat to Akron, Ohio, my hometown. But that was all I had basically. And the story so fascinated me that I tried to write about it. I started off writing stories about my grandfather and soon, because I ran out of real fact, in order to keep going, I made up facts for this character, Thomas . . . then this poem "Dusting" appeared, really out of nowhere. I didn't realize this was Thomas's wife saying "I want to talk and you can't do this side without my side. . . ."[5]

The poems combine family history with American history. In the first part of this century, many southern blacks moved to northern industrial cities. Dove's poem tells the story of a midwestern African-American married couple, from 1900 to 1960. Thomas journeys from the rural South to the industrial city of Akron, where he finds work in a Goodyear Zeppelin factory. He later loses his job because of the Depression.

In the sequence of poems, each life is vividly portrayed. Dove writes about apparently unimportant times in her grandparents' lives. With her immense talent, the poet relates these moments to American history.

In *Thomas and Beulah*, Dove showed her striking ability to write from different points of view. The book's first section is in Thomas's voice. The second part relates his wife's experience.

Dove writes about a startlingly wide range of topics. "Obviously as a black woman, I am concerned with race . . . But certainly not every poem of mine mentions the fact of being black. . . . They are poems about humanity, and sometimes humanity happens to be black. I cannot run from, I *won't* run from any kind of truth."[6]

Dove has a long list of literary honors. Her poetry has earned her fellowships from the National

Endowment for the Arts, the Guggenheim Foundation, and the National Humanities Center, among others. She was granted a Portia Pittman fellowship from the National Endowment for the Humanities as writer-in-residence at Tuskegee Institute in 1982. She was chosen by Robert Penn Warren—then the first U.S. Poet Laureate—to receive a 1986 Lavan Younger Poet Award from the Academy of American Poets. She received a Literary Lion citation from the New York Public Library in 1990.

Dove has read her poetry on several national television and radio shows. She filmed a segment with Big Bird for *Sesame Street.* The poet hosted and produced *Shine Up Your Words: A Morning with Rita Dove,* a nationally televised one-hour program about poetry, featuring elementary school children. Dove serves as editor of *Callahoo,* the preeminent magazine for African-American arts and literature. She is an advisory editor and board member of several journals.

Dove taught creative writing at Arizona State University from 1981 to 1989. Since then, she has taught at the University of Virginia, Charlottesville (UVA). At UVA she holds the chair as a Commonwealth Professor of English. Dove is a commissioner of the Schomburg Center for Research in Black Culture, part of the New York Public Library.

Dove's poem "The Zeppelin Factory" is a fine piece from *Thomas and Beulah.*

The Zeppelin Factory

The zeppelin factory
needed workers, all right—
but, standing in the cage
of the whale's belly, sparks
flying off the joints
and noise thundering,
Thomas wanted to sit
right down and cry.

That spring the third
largest airship was dubbed
the biggest joke
in town, though they all
turned out for the launch.
Wind caught,
"The Akron" floated
out of control,
three men in tow—
one dropped
to safety, one
hung on but the third,
muscles and adrenalin
failing, fell
clawing
six hundred feet.

Thomas at night
in the vacant lot:
*Here I am, intact
and faint-hearted.*

Thomas hiding
his heart with his hat
at the football game, eyeing
the Goodyear blimp overhead:
*Big boy I know
you're in there.*

Chapter Notes

Introduction

1. Henry Louis Gates, Jr., *Figures in Black: Words, Signs, & the "Racial" Self* (New York: Oxford University Press, 1987), p. xxvi.

Chapter 1

1. Margarita Matilda Odell, *Memoir* (Boston: 1834), p. 12.

2. George Perkins, Sculley Bradley, Richmond Croom Beatty, E. Hudson Long, eds., *The American Tradition in Literature*, 6th ed. (New York: Random House, 1985), vol. 2, p. 224.

3. Odell, p. 12.

4. Phillis Wheatley, *The Collected Works of Phillis Wheatley*, ed. John Shields (New York: Oxford University Press, 1988), p. 24.

Chapter 2

1. Mabel M. Smythe, ed., *The Black American Reference Book* (Englewood Cliffs, N.J.: Prentice Hall, 1976), p. 48.

2. James Weldon Johnson, *Book of American Negro Poetry* (Orlando, FLa.: Harcourt, Brace and World, 1922), p. 34.

3. Ashley Bryan, *I Greet the Dawn: Poems by Paul Laurence Dunbar* (New York: Atheneum, 1978), p. 7.

4. Nikki Giovanni, in *Contemporary Authors* (Detroit: Gale Research, 1988), vol. 124, p. 122.

Chapter 3

1. George Perkins, Sculley Bradley, Richmond Croom Beatty, and E. Hudson Long, eds., *The American Tradition in Literature*, 6th ed. (New York: Random House, 1985), vol. 2, p. 1374.

2. Langston Hughes, in *African American Literature: Voices in a Tradition* (Austin, Tex.: Holt, Rinehart and Winston, 1992), p. 312.

3. Langston Hughes in Perkins et al., p. 1374.

Chapter 4

1. Martha Liebrum, in *Contemporary Authors*, New Revision Series (Detroit: Gale Research, 1962), vol. 1, p. 74.

2. Alice Walker, in *The Norton Anthology of American Literature*, 3rd ed. (New York: W.W. Norton & Co., 1989), p. 2503.

3. Carl H. Klaus, Robert Scholes, Nancy R. Comley, and Michael Silverman, eds., *Elements of Literature* (New York: Oxford University Press, 1986), p. 725.

4. Walker, p. 2504.

5. Ibid., p. 2503.

6. Gwendolyn Brooks, in *Contemporary Authors,* New Revision Series (Detroit: Gale Reasearch, 1962), vol. 1, p. 75.

Chapter 5

1. Amiri Baraka, in *The Norton Anthology of American Literature*, 3rd ed., (New York: W.W. Norton & Co., 1989), vol. 2, p. 2744.

2. Amiri Baraka, in *African American Literature: Voices in a Tradition* (Austin, Tex.: Holt, Rinehart and Winston, 1992), p. 679.

3. Stephen Schenck, in *Contemporary Authors* (Detroit: Gale Research, 1977), vol. 21–24, p. 456.

Chapter 6

1. Haki R. Madhubuti, in *Contemporary Authors,* New Revision Series (Detroit: Gale Research, 1988), vol. 24, p. 295.

2. Haki R. Madhubuti, *Claiming Earth: Race, Rape, Ritual, Richness in America & the Search for Enlightened Empowerment* (Chicago: Third World Press, 1994), p. 9.

3. Ibid.

4. Madhubuti, in *Contemporary Authors*, p. 295.

5. Haki R. Madhubuti, *Don't Cry, Scream* (Chicago: Third World Press, 1969), p. 9.

Chapter 7

1. Nikki Giovanni, *Racism 101* (New York: William Morrow, 1995), p. 181.

2. Nikki Giovanni, in Sally Holtze, *Fifth Book of Junior Authors & Illustrators* (New York: H.W. Wilson, 1983), p. 134.

3. Arlene Clift Pellow, in Jessie Smith, ed., *Notable Black American Women* (Detroit: Gale Research, 1992), p. 404.

4. Peter Bailey, "Nikki Giovanni: 'I Am Black, Female, Polite...'" *Ebony*, February 1972, p. 49.

5. Ida Lewis, in the foreword to Nikki Giovanni, *My House* (New York: William Morrow, 1972), pp. ix–xv.

Chapter 8

1. Lynn Z. Bloom, "Maya Angelou," in *African-American Writers After 1955: Dramatists & Prose Writers*, ed. Thadious M. Davis and Trudier Harris (Detroit: Gale Research, 1985), p. 13.

2. Maya Angelou, *I Know Why the Caged Bird Sings* (New York: Random House, 1970), p. 2.

3. M.F.K. Fisher, in Maya Angelou, *Oh Pray My Wings Are Gonna Fit Me Well* (New York: Random House, 1975), p. 1.

4. James Baldwin, in Maya Angelou, *Just Give Me a Cool Drink of Water 'Fore I Diiie* (New York: Random House, 1971), back cover.

Chapter 9

1. Eloise Greenfield, in Sally Holtze, *Fifth Book of Junior Authors & Illustrators* (New York: H.W. Wilson, 1983), p. 137.

2. Eloise Greenfield, in *Something About the Author* (Detroit: Gale Research, 1980), p. 143.

3. Ibid., p. 143.

4. Eloise Greenfield, "Something to Shout About," speech given at the International Reading Association–Children's Book Council Preconvention Institute, "Books Open Minds," May 23, 1975, New York, N.Y.

5. Audrey Eaglen, "Black and Beautiful," *Top of the News*, Winter 1980, p. 224.

6. Jacqueline Trescott, "Children's Books and Heroes," *The Washington Post*, October 29, 1976, p. B5, Col. 4.

7. Eloise Greenfield, in Holtze, p. 138.

Chapter 10

1. Rita Dove, *The Poet's World* (Washington, D.C.: The Library of Congress, 1995), p. 75.

2. Ibid., p. 76.

3. Ibid.

4. Rita Dove, in *African American Literature: Voices in a Tradition* (Austin, Tex.: Holt Rinehart and Winston, 1992), p. 717.

5. Rita Dove, in *The Norton Anthology of American Literature*, 3rd ed., (New York: W.W. Norton & Co., 1989), p. 2772.

6. Rita Dove, in *African American Literature*, p. 717.

Further Reading

Works by Phillis Wheatley

Collected Works of Phillis Wheatley. New York: Oxford University Press, Incorporated, 1989.

Memoir & Poems of Phillis Wheatley, a Native African & a Slave. Temecula, Calif.: Ayer Company Publishers, 1977.

The Poems of Phillis Wheatley. Chapel Hill: University of North Carolina Press, 1989.

Poems on Various Subjects, Religious & Moral. New York: A M S Press, Inc.

Works About Phillis Wheatley

Richmond, Merle. *Phyllis Wheatley.* New York: Chelsea House Publishers, 1988.

Works by Paul Laurence Dunbar

Best Stories of Paul Laurence Dunbar. Temecula, Calif: Reprint Services, Corporation, 1992.

The Collected Poetry of Paul Laurence Dunbar. Charlottesville: University Press of Virginia, 1993.

The Complete Poems of Paul Laurence Dunbar. Philadelphia: Hakim's Publishers, 1993.

Lyrics of Love & Laughter. Temecula, Calif: Reprint Services Corporation, 1993.

Lyrics of a Lowly Life. Temecula, Calif: Reprint Services Corporation, 1992.

Majors & Minors. Temecula, Calif: Reprint Services, Corporation, 1992.

Oak & Ivy. Temecula, Calif: Reprint Services, Corporation, 1992.

Works About Paul Laurence Dunbar

Gentry, Tony. *Paul L. Dunbar.* New York: Chelsea House Publishers, 1989.

Dunbar, Paul L. *Life & Works of Paul Laurence Dunbar.* Nashville: Winston-Derek Publishers, 1992.

Revell, Peter. *Paul Laurence Dunbar.* New York: Macmillan Library Reference, 1979.

Works by Langston Hughes

Poetry

Collected Poems of Langston Hughes. New York Random House, 1995.

The Dream Keeper: And Other Poems. New York: Alfred A. Knopf Books for Young Readers, 1994.

The Langston Hughes Reader. New York: George Braziller, 1981.

Selected Poems of Langston Hughes. New York: Alfred A. Knopf, 1959.

Other Works

The Best of Semple. New York: Farrar, Straus & Giroux, 1990.

The Big Sea: An Autobiography. New York: Hill & Wang, Incorporated, 1993.

I Wonder As I Wander: An Autobiographical Journey. New York: Hill & Wang, 1993.

Mule Bone: A Comedy of Negro Life in Three Acts. New York: HarperCollins Publishers, 1991.

Not Without Laughter. New York: Macmillan, 1986.

Short Stories. New York: Hill & Wang, 1996.

Works About Langston Hughes

Dunham, Montrew. *Childhood of Famous Americans Langston Hughes: Young Black Poet.* New York: Simon & Schuster Children's, 1995.

Berry, S. L. *Langston Hughes.* New York: Creative Education, 1994.

Haskins, James S. *Always Movin' On: The Life of Langston Hughes.* New York: Africa World Press, 1992.

Rummel, Jack. *Langston Hughes*. New York: Chelsea House Publishers, 1989.

Works by Gwendolyn Brooks

Annie Allen. Westport, Conn.: Greenwood Publishing Group, 1972.

Blacks. Chicago: Third World Press, 1991.

Bronzeville Boys & Girls. New York: HarperCollins Children's Books, 1967.

A Capsule Course in Black Poetry Writing. Detroit: Broadside Press, 1975.

Maud Martha. Chicago: Third World Press, 1993.

The Near Johannesburg Boy & Other Poems. Chicago: Third World Press, 1991.

Report from Part One: An Autobiography. Detroit: Broadside Press, 1972.

Report from Part Two. Chicago: Third World Press, 1996.

Selected Poems. New York: HarperCollins Publishers, 1982.

To Disembark. Chicago: Third World Press, 1981.

Works About Gwendolyn Brooks

Gwendolyn Brooks: Poet. New York: Chelsea House Publishers, 1995.

Madhubuti, Haki R. ed. *Say That the River Turns: The Impact of Gwendolyn Brooks*. Chicago: Third World Press, 1987.

Works by Amiri Baraka

The Autobiography of LeRoi Jones. Chicago: Lawrence Hill Books, 1994.

Black Music. Westport, Conn. Greenwood Publishing Group, 1980.

LeRoi Jones-Amiri Baraka Reader. New York: Thunder's Mouth Press, 1991.

Shy's, Wise, Y's: The Griot's Tale. Third World Press, 1994.

Transbluesency: The Selected Poems of Amiri Baraka Leroi Jones. New York: Marsilio Publishers, 1995.

Works About Amiri Baraka

Bernotas, Bob. *Amiri Baraka (Le Roi Jones).* New York: Chelsea House Publishers, 1991.

Reilly, Charlie. ed. *Conversations with Amiri Baraka.* Jackson: University Press of Mississippi, 1994.

Works by Haki R. Madhubuti

Book of Life. Chicago: Third World Press, 1992.

Don't Cry, Scream. Chicago: Third World Press, 1992.

Killing Memory, Seeking Ancestors. Chicago: Third World Press, 1987.

Works by Nikki Giovanni

Black Feeling, Black Talk/Black Judgement. New York: William Morrow & Company, 1971.

Cotton Candy on a Rainy Day. New York: William Morrow & Company, Incorporated, 1980.

Ego-Tripping & Other Poems for Young People. Chicago: Lawrence Hill Books, 1993.

Gemini: An Extended Autobiographical Statement on My First Twenty-Five Years of Being a Black Poet. New York: Viking Penguin, 1976.

The Genie in the Jar. New York: Henry Holt & Company, 1996.

Grand Mothers. New York: Henry Holt & Company, 1994.

Knoxville, Tennessee. New York: Scholastic, 1994.

My House. New York: William Morrow & Company, 1974.

Racism 101. New York: William Morrow & Company, 1995.

The Selected Poems of Nikki Giovanni. New York: William Morrow & Company, 1996.

Spin a Soft Black Song. Farrar, Straus & Giroux, 1985.

Vacation Time: Poems for Children. New York: William Morrow & Company, 1981.

The Women and the Men. New York: William Morrow & Company, 1979.

Works About Nikki Giovanni

Fowler, Virginia C. *Nikki Giovanni.* New York: Macmillan Library Reference, 1992.

Works by Maya Angleou

Poetry

And Still I Rise. New York: Random House, 1978.

A Brave & Startling Truth. New York: Random House, 1995.

The Complete Collected Poems of Maya Angelou. New York: Random House, 1994.

Just Give Me A Cool Drink of Water 'Fore I Diiie. New York: Random House, 1971.

On the Pulse of Morning. New York: Random House, 1993.

Poems: Maya Angelou. New York: Bantam Books, Incorporated, 1986.

Wouldn't Take Nothing for My Journey Now. New York: Bantam Books, Incorporated, 1994.

Autobiographical Works

All God's Children Need Traveling Shoes. New York: Bandom Books, 1986.

Gather Together in My Name. New York: Bantam Books, 1985.

Heart of a Woman. New York: Bantam Books, 1984.

I Know Why the Caged Bird Sings. New York: Bantam Books, Incorporated, 1983.

Singin' & Swingin' & Gettin' Merry Like Christmas. New York: Bantam Books, 1985.

Works About Maya Angelou

Lisandrelli, Elaine S. *Maya Angelou: More Than a Poet.* Springfield, N.J.: Enslow Publishers, 1996.

Shapiro, Miles. *Maya Angelou, Author.* New York: Chelsea House Publishers, 1994.

Works by Eloise Greenfield

Africa Dream. New York: HarperCollins Children's Books, 1989.

For the Love of the Game: Michael Jordan & Me. New York: HarperCollins Publishers, 1995.

Honey, I Love & Other Love Poems. New York: HarperCollins Children's Books, 1978.

Nathaniel Talking. New York: Writers & Readers Publishing, 1988.

Night on Neighborhood Street. New York: Dial Books for Young Readers, 1991.

She Come Bringing Me That Little Baby Girl. New York: HarperCollins Children's Books, 1974.

Under the Sunday Tree. New York: HarperCollins Children's Books, 1988.

Works by Rita Dove

Grace Notes: Poems. New York: W. W. Norton & Company, 1991.

Mother Love. New York: W. W. Norton & Company, 1995. *Museum.* Pittsburgh: Carnegie-Mellon University Press, 1983.

Selected Poems. New York: Random House, 1993.

Thomas & Beulah. Pittsburgh: Carnegie-Mellon University Press, 1985.

The Yellow House on the Corner. Pittsburgh: Carnegie-Mellon University Press, 1989.

Index